Animal Bodies

WHOSE EARS ARE THOSE?

By Mary Griffin

Gareth Stevens
PUBLISHING

Please visit our website, www.garethstevens.com. For a free color catalog of all our high-quality books, call toll free 1-800-542-2595 or fax 1-877-542-2596.

Library of Congress Cataloging-in-Publication Data

Names: Griffin, Mary, 1978- author.
Title: Whose ears are those? / Mary Griffin.
Description: New York : Gareth Stevens Publishing, [2024] | Series: Animal bodies | Includes index.
Identifiers: LCCN 2022046875 (print) | LCCN 2022046876 (ebook) | ISBN 9781538286357 (library binding) | ISBN 9781538286340 (paperback) | ISBN 9781538286364 (ebook)
Subjects: LCSH: Ear–Juvenile literature.
Classification: LCC QL948 .G837 2024 (print) | LCC QL948 (ebook) | DDC 591.4/4–dc23/eng/20221003
LC record available at https://lccn.loc.gov/2022046875
LC ebook record available at https://lccn.loc.gov/2022046876

Published in 2024 by
Gareth Stevens Publishing
2544 Clinton Street
Buffalo, NY 14224

Designer: Tanya Dellaccio Keeney
Editor: Therese Shea

Photo credits: Cover, p. 1 Rolf E. Staerk/Shutterstock.com; pp. 5, 7 Rita_Kochmarjova/ Shutterstock.com; pp. 9, 11 Michal van den Berg/Shutterstock.com; pp. 13, 15 Pooja Prasanth/ Shutterstock.com; p. 17 Yatra4289 /Shutterstock.com; p 19 nattanan726/Shutterstock.com; pp. 21, 23 Rudmer Zwerver/Shutterstock.com.

Printed in the United States of America

CPSIA compliance information: Batch #CSGS24: For further information contact Gareth Stevens, at 1-800-542-2595.

Find us on

Contents

Let's look at animal ears!
Look at these long ears.

5

It's a rabbit!
Its ears catch sound waves.

Look at these pointy ears.

9

It's a fox!
It can move its ears
to find a sound.

Look at this huge ear.

13

It's an elephant!
Its ears keep it cool.

Look at this fluffy ear.

It's a koala!
Its ears have fur
inside and outside.

Look at these tall ears.

It's a bat!
It listens for bugs.
It eats them!